Simple Vegan Comfort Food

From the Café Indigo Kitchen

Chili, page 39

Simple Vegan Comfort Food

From the
Café Indigo Kitchen

PATTI DANN

PHOTOGRAPHY BY JOSHUA SWEENY

FOOD STYLING, ADDITIONAL PHOTOGRAPHY
BY LAURIE KNOOP

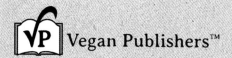 Vegan Publishers™

Vegan Publishers
Danvers, Massachusetts
www.veganpublishers.com

© 2019 by Patti Dann
Photographs © 2019 by Joshua Sweeny

ISBN: 978-1-940184-56-2

Food styling by Laurie Knoop
Design & typesetting by David Dann Studio

Corn & Black Bean
Salsa, page 47

Contents

Scenes from Café Indigo

CAFÉ INDIGO

In life, we all have decisions to make. For us, the fork in the road came when we found ourselves deciding whether to focus our energy on our beloved café, **Café Indigo**, or to focus more intentionally on our growing cadre of grandchildren. It wasn't an easy decision. We often thought that we could do it all, but we found it particularly tough because we had made so many friends – friends that loved the delicious vegan food we made for their enjoyment. In the end, we chose the joy of spending time with our seven grandchildren over the retail operation of **Café Indigo**. It was a smart choice.

Since our retail location closed, we've heard regularly from our former customers lamenting that they can no longer enjoy one of our famous brunches, one of our delicious vegan cheesesteaks, or a delectable Rachael Sandwich. We felt for our friends and former customers. Before long, we started talking about the possibility of sharing our many wonderful vegan options in the form of a cookbook. What better way to

share the joy of **Café Indigo** with our friends, former customers, and the world?

The mission of **Café Indigo** was to make delicious vegan food that everyone could enjoy. This cookbook continues this tradition but provides you with the opportunity to be the chef. Throughout the book, we present you with the finest recipes from **Café Indigo's Vegan Goodness Café**. You'll find the recipe for our famous vegan cheesesteak, the seitan recipe to make the Rachael Sandwich, as well as our famous holiday roast. You'll find everything you

need to make your own Sunday brunch and delicious deserts. Our signature cakes, found in high quality markets throughout the country, will forever remain a family secret.

Many people helped with the creation of *Simple Vegan Comfort Food*, and we would like to acknowledge them here. First, our three beautiful daughters, who introduced us to the goodness of veganism, and their children, our grandkids, who continue to make preparing vegan treats a delight. Photographer Joshua Sweeny made our dishes look as good as they taste and stylist Laurie Knoop gave those images a homey, warm look. Designer David Dann made these recipes easy to read and appealing, and our editor at Vegan Publishers, Casey Taft, helped make this cookbook become a reality.

We hope you enjoy the recipes and, if you feel the urge to reach out to us, don't hesitate to contact us at **cafeindigo.com**.

Patti Dann

'Vegan cuisine can be easy to prepare and wonderfully flavorful. I know, because at Café Indigo we never served a dull meal!' – Patti Dann

---

Chapter 1

CAFÉ BASICS

This section contains our seitan, tofu, tempeh "bacon," and other basics you will need for many of the recipes in this book. These can all be made in advance and frozen so they are ready when you have a craving for a Rachael, a grilled seitan wrap, or a TBLT.

OUR ORIGINAL SEITAN
Makes 1 roll | Serves 8

3 cups vital wheat gluten

3 tablespoons soy flour

1/2 cup nutritional yeast

2 teaspoons paprika

1 teaspoon sea salt

3 tablespoons onion powder

3 tablespoon garlic powder

1 teaspoon black pepper

2 tablespoons tamari

1/2 cup canola oil

3/4 cup pureed white beans

2 cups water

ALTHOUGH WE HAVE recently created a newer, simpler seitan recipe, this is the original seitan we made and sold at our café. It is the main ingredient in our famous Rachael sandwich, and our ever popular grilled seitan wrap and pepper steak sandwich.

Preheat oven to 350F.

Place the dry ingredients into a mixing bowl and whisk everything together. Add the remaining ingredients and mix well, using a mixer on low/medium, for 1 to 2 minutes.

As soon as threads appear, stop mixing. Do not overmix or the dough will become tough. Remove the dough from the bowl and press into a rectangle, about 6" x 8."

Starting at the smaller side, roll up to form a log. Wrap tightly in foil, making sure to wrap the foil twice around. Place directly on the oven rack.

Bake for one hour. Turn the roll over and bake for another hour.

Remove seitan from the oven and let cool before removing the foil.

Slice the seitan into 1/2-inch rounds and pan fry in a lightly oiled pan for 2 to 3 minutes per side.

Slices can be frozen and used later.

To make crumbles: Place 3 to 4 slices into the food processor and pulse until the seitan breaks down into smaller pieces. Be careful not to process for too long or you will end up with crumbs. Use crumbles in dishes like tacos, chili, and stuffed peppers.

To make cutlets: Take a golf ball sized piece of dough, knead it for 1 minute and flatten, pushing the dough away from the center to form a flat cutlet. When all the cutlets are made, add one at a time to a pot of boiling water, or you can use broth for extra flavor. Simmer for 45 minutes. Use a slotted spoon to remove the cutlets from the water. When the cutlets are cool, gently squeeze out the excess liquid.

CAFÉ TIP
Use immediately or store in an airtight container in the refrigerator or freezer.

THE NEW SEITAN

Makes 1 roll | Serves 6

1 lb. package silken tofu

1 1/2 cups pureed white beans

1 tablespoon vegetable broth paste

2 cups vital wheat gluten

WE CAME UP WITH this recipe when we were trying to recreate a seitan/tofu snack that our grandchildren had eaten somewhere and nicknamed "chewy" tofu. We never quite mastered the chewy tofu part, but we ended up with a seitan recipe that was lighter than our original seitan. This is very simple to make and has become a favorite in our house.

Preheat the oven to 350F.

Drain and crumble the tofu and place it into the food processor. Add the beans and broth paste and process until smooth.

Transfer to a mixing bowl. Add the vital wheat gluten and mix until combined and the dough appears thread-like. Be careful not to overmix.

To make 1 loaf of seitan, form the dough into a log about 8-inches long. Wrap tightly in aluminum foil. Place the log directly on the oven rack and bake for 50 minutes. Turn the roll over and bake another 50 minutes.

Remove from the oven and let cool before unwrapping.

To make cutlets: Pull off golf ball sized sections of the seitan, roll into a ball, flatten, and set aside. When all the cutlets are ready, add one at a time into a pot of boiling water, or broth for extra flavor, waiting 30 seconds between each addition to keep them from sticking together. After they have all been added, turn the heat down and let the cutlets simmer for 30 minutes. Remove, using a slotted spoon, and let cool.

To make a gluten-free version: Substitute the vital wheat gluten with 1 7/8 cups rice flour, 1/8 cup potato flour and 1 1/2 teaspoons xanthan gum.

ORIGINAL GLUTEN-FREE SEITAN

Makes 1 roll | Serves 6

2 cups rice flour

2 1/2 tablespoons
potato flour

2 teaspoon xanthan gum

2 1/2 tablespoons
tapioca flour

1/3 cup nutritional yeast

1 1/2 teaspoon paprika

2 1/2 tablespoons
onion powder

2 1/2 tablespoon
garlic powder

1 1/2 teaspoons pepper

2 1/2 tablespoons
wheat-free tamari

1/3 cup canola oil

1 cup water

1/2 cup pureed white beans

WE CREATED THIS gluten-free version of our seitan for our GF family and friends. This version is more fragile than Our Original Seitan recipe, so slice, using a serrated knife, to gently cut the roll. Save any pieces that break apart to use in our Lentil Burgers (page 51).

Preheat the oven to 350F.

Place all of the ingredients into a mixing bowl and mix on medium until a dough forms. Remove from the mixer and form it into a roll.

Wrap the roll tightly in foil and bake for one hour. Flip over and bake for another 50 minutes. Allow the roll to cool before unwrapping.

Carefully slice and pan fry in a small amount of oil.

Tofu Bacon & Tempeh Bacon

Makes 12 to 18 slices

2 8oz. packages of tempeh or 1 lb. extra firm tofu

1/2 cup water

2 tablespoons tamari

1 tablespoon maple syrup

1 teaspoon olive oil

1/2 teaspoon garlic powder

1/4 teaspoon liquid smoke, optional

I LOVE TOFU, but tempeh was never a favorite, so I decided to start seasoning tempeh the same way I prepare tofu and now I love it.

Preheat the oven to 350F.

Thinly slice the tempeh or tofu.

In a small bowl, mix together the water, tamari, maple syrup, olive oil, garlic powder, and liquid smoke, if using.

Place the tofu or tempeh in a large baking dish and pour the marinade over the slices. Let it sit for 10 minutes to marinate.

Bake for 30 minutes.

You can also cook the tofu or tempeh bacon in a skillet over medium heat. Add a small amount of oil and cook for 4 to 5 minutes per side until most of the marinade has been absorbed.

Basic Cheese Sauce

Makes 6 cups of sauce

1/4 cup Earth Balance

2 tablespoons grated onion

3 cups soy milk, divided into 2 portions of 1 1/2 cups each

3/4 cup cashew butter

1 cup pureed pumpkin

1/2 cup nutritional yeast

1/2 teaspoon Dijon mustard

1 teaspoon lemon juice

1/2 teaspoon garlic powder

1/2 teaspoon paprika

1 cup of your favorite vegan cheese, optional

THIS CHEESE SAUCE can be used as the basis for a number of delicious vegan dishes, including everyone's favorite, Mac & Cheese (see the recipe on page 59).

Sauté the grated onion in the Earth Balance for 3-4 minutes.

Add 1 1/2 cups of soy milk, cashew butter, pumpkin, nutritional yeast, Dijon mustard, lemon juice garlic powder and paprika. Whisk together until smooth. Add the remaining 1 1/2 cups of soy milk and whisk until smooth.

Stir in the 1 cup of vegan cheese, if you are using it.

Faux Turkey

Faux Turkey

Makes 1 roll | Serves 6 to 8

1 New Seitan recipe, page 15, rolled into a rectangle about 6″ x 8″

Stuffing Mixture

1/2 loaf of bread, sourdough, baguette or your favorite bread, torn into small pieces

1/3 cup diced onion

1/3 cup diced celery

2 tablespoons poultry seasoning

1/2 cup water

THIS IS OUR holiday roll that we served during our Holiday Brunch every November. Use leftovers to make a great sandwich. The stuffing is a basic bread stuffing, but you can substitute with your favorite as long as it isn't a wet stuffing because if the stuffing is too wet, the inside of the roll will not cook properly.

Preheat the oven to 350F.

Make the seitan recipe. Pan fry 1 side only, over medium heat, until lightly browned. Remove from heat and set aside.

To make the stuffing, add the bread to a mixing bowl. Add the onion and celery, poultry seasoning, and mix together. Pour the water over the mixture and, using your hands, mix together until all of the bread is moist.

Place the seitan, cooked side up, on a clean surface. Press the stuffing into the dough, leaving a 1/2-inch border on the top and sides. Roll into a log and pinch the ends together. Wrap tightly in foil, with the foil wrapping around the log twice.

Place directly on the oven rack and bake for 75 minutes. Turn over and bake for another hour.

To make a gluten free version: Use the gluten free seitan recipe and substitute gluten-free bread in the stuffing.

Soysage Mix

Makes 24 to 30 Soysage patties

2 1/3 cup textured vegetable protein (TVP)

1/4 cup oats

2 cups boiling water

1 tablespoon nutritional yeast

1 1/2 teaspoons onion powder

1 1/2 teaspoons garlic powder

1/2 teaspoon balsamic vinegar

1/3 cup olive oil

2 tablespoons maple syrup

3 tablespoons tamari

1 to 2 cups bread crumbs

1/2 teaspoon liquid smoke, optional

WE ALWAYS SERVED these "sausage" patties at our Sunday brunch. We also used them in our ever popular spinach and Soysage quesadilla and burrito. They also make a great addition to pasta sauce and chili.

Preheat the oven to 350F. Line a baking sheet with parchment paper.

Place the TVP and oats in a mixing bowl, pour in the hot water, stir, and let sit for 30 minutes.

Add the mixture, along with the remaining ingredients, into the bowl of a food processor and mix for 3 to 5 minutes on medium.

To make Soysages, form the mixture into small patties, using 2 tablespoons of the mixture, and place on the baking sheet.

Bake for 15 minutes. Flip over and bake for another 10 minutes.

Basil Dressing

Makes 18 ounces of dressing

1 cup olive oil

1/4 cup red wine vinegar

1/4 cup balsamic vinegar

1/2 cup sugar

1/4 cup fresh basil, finely chopped

1 cloves garlic, minced

2 teaspoons lemon juice

Salt & pepper to taste

Whisk the oil, vinegars and sugar in bowl until well blended.

Add in the fresh basil, garlic, lemon juice and season to taste.

Serve over tossed greens, sliced tomatoes, peppers, onions, cucumbers and other salad ingredients.

Basil Dressing

Cornmeal Pancakes,
page 24

Chapter 2

BRUNCH AT THE CAFÉ

In this section, we have included recipes from our famous holiday and Mother's Day brunches. Even though our café is closed, and we don't serve brunch anymore, it doesn't mean that you can't recreate the experience in your own home.

CORNMEAL PANCAKES

Serves 6

1 cup cornmeal

1 tablespoon sugar

1 teaspoon salt

1 cup boiling water

1/2 cup soy milk

1 tablespoon canola oil

1/2 cup flour

2 teaspoons baking powder

In a large bowl, mix together the cornmeal, sugar, salt, and boiling water. Cover and let sit for 10 minutes.

Stir in the soy milk, oil, and flour and mix well. Gently stir in the baking powder.

Cook on preheated griddle, 3 minutes per side.

To make cornmeal waffles: Add 1/4 cup flour to the above recipe.

CINNAMON FRENCH TOAST

Serves 6

Vegan Buttermilk

1 cup vanilla soy milk

1 tablespoon apple cider vinegar

1/4 cup chickpea flour

1 tablespoon sugar

2 teaspoons cinnamon

2 tablespoon canola oil

Maple syrup

6 slices of our cinnamon bread, sliced 1-inch thick

To make the buttermilk, whisk together the soy milk and cider vinegar. Set aside to acidulate.

Whisk together the chickpea flour, sugar, and cinnamon.

Pour the buttermilk into the flour mixture and whisk together.

Heat a skillet with a tablespoon of oil. Dip a slice of cinnamon bread in the batter, letting the excess drip off. Place in the skillet, repeating with as many slices that will fit in your skillet, but don't crowd the pan. Cook until lightly browned on each side, about 3 to 4 minutes per side. Repeat until all of the slice are done.

Serve with maple syrup.

ORIGINAL BAKED TOFU SCRAM

Makes 8 servings

1 lb. package firm or extra firm tofu

2 teaspoons onion powder

2 teaspoons garlic powder

1/4 teaspoon salt

1/2 teaspoon turmeric

2 tablespoon nutritional yeast

Preheat your oven to 350F.

Crumble the tofu into a large bowl. Add the onion powder, garlic powder, salt, turmeric, nutritional yeast, mix well. Add 1 cup of your favorite chopped vegetables such as onions, peppers, carrots, and mushrooms

Bake for 45 minutes.

THE NEW SCRAM

Makes 8 servings

1 lb. package firm tofu

1 box of silken firm tofu

2 teaspoons onion powder

2 teaspoons garlic powder

1/4 teaspoon salt

1/2 teaspoon turmeric

2 tablespoons nutritional yeast

Preheat the oven to 350F.

Drain the water from the tofus and crumble in a large bowl. Add the onion powder, garlic powder, salt, turmeric, nutritional yeast, and oil. Mix well.

Bake for 45 minutes.

Sesame Noodles

Makes 8 servings

Sauce

1 head of roasted garlic, half of it mashed

1/3 cup tahini

1/2 cup tamari

1/4 cup balsamic vinegar

1/3 cup maple syrup

1/3 cup toasted sesame oil

1 teaspoon Sriracha

2/3 cup canola oil

Assembly

1 package Pad Thai noodles

2 tablespoons roasted sesame seeds

Chopped cilantro, for garnish

THESE WERE ALWAYS on the brunch table. It seemed like we could never make enough. The secret? Roasted garlic.

To roast the garlic, cut off the top of the head of garlic to expose the bulbs. Pour 1 teaspoon of olive oil over the top. Wrap in foil and bake at 400F for 25 to 30 minutes.

Mash half of the head of roasted garlic and add to the sauce.

Mix the sauce together in a small bowl. Set aside.

Prepare the Pad Thai noodles according to the package instructions.

Drain the noodles and toss with the marinade. Sprinkle with sesame seeds and cilantro.

Oven Roasted Brunch Potatoes

Makes 6 to 8 servings

Marinade

1 cup olive oil

1/4 cup fresh lemon juice

1 tablespoon Dijon mustard

1 teaspoon salt

1 tablespoon garlic powder

1 tablespoon rosemary

1 teaspoon black pepper

6 medium to large red potatoes

Preheat the oven to 400F.

Mix together the marinade. Wash and dice the potatoes.

Toss the potatoes in the marinade and let them sit for 15 minutes.

Using a slotted spoon, transfer the potatoes to a baking sheet. Pour remaining marinade over the potatoes.

Bake for 30 to 40 minutes.

Sesame Noodles

STUFFED MUSHROOMS

Makes 12

18 mushrooms

1 tablespoon olive oil

1/4 cup onion, finely chopped

1 tablespoon tamari

1 teaspoon vegan Worcestershire sauce

1/4 cup fresh bread crumbs

MOM WOULD MAKE these stuffed mushrooms for special occasions. We loved them so much that we started serving them as an appetizer at our holiday brunch. Then we started making them for our Mother's Day brunch. Then we started making them all the time! Why wait for a special occasion? Use your favorite mushrooms. I like to mix button mushrooms with baby bellas.

Preheat oven to 350F.

Wash the mushrooms and remove the stems. Place 12 of the mushrooms, inside side up, in a baking dish.

Heat oil in a skillet. Chop the remaining mushrooms, either by hand or in the food processor, and add them to the skillet. Add the onions. Sauté for 5 to 8 minutes, until the mushrooms and onions are soft.

Turn off the heat and add the tamari, Worcestershire sauce, and bread crumbs.

When the stuffing has cooled, add 1 tablespoon of stuffing to each of the 12 mushrooms. Place them, stuffing side up, in a baking pan.

Add 2 tablespoons of water to the bottom of the pan and bake for 30 minutes.

HUMMUS

Makes 6 to 8 servings

1 clove garlic

6 black olives, pitted

1/4 cup tahini

2 cups chickpeas

1/2 teaspoon salt

2 tablespoons fresh lemon juice

2 tablespoons water

2 tablespoons olive oil

Place all ingredients in food processor and process until smooth.

Butternut Squash with Apples

Makes 6 to 8 servings

1/2 cup vegan butter

1/2 cup maple syrup

1/4 cup apple cider

1 teaspoon ground cinnamon

1/2 teaspoon ground allspice

1/4 teaspoon nutmeg

2 small butternut squashes, peeled, seeded, and cut into slices, about 4 cups

5 Granny Smith apples, cut into slices, about 4 cups

THIS WAS ONE of the casseroles that was served during our holiday brunch every November. Prepping a butternut squash is time consuming, so buy the squash already peeled and sliced, to make it easier.

Preheat oven to 400F. Lightly oil a baking dish.

Melt the butter and add it to a large mixing bowl. Add the maple syrup, apple cider, and spices. Set aside.

Prep the squash and apples and add to the butter mixture. Stir to coat.

Cover with foil and bake for 1 hour or until the squash is tender.

Pea Salad

Makes 5 servings

3 cups frozen peas

1/2 cup thinly sliced red onion

1 cup silken tofu

1 1/2 teaspoon apple cider vinegar

1 1/2 teaspoon fresh lemon juice

1/2 teaspoon Dijon mustard

1/2 teaspoon sea salt

1/2 teaspoon black pepper

MY MOM HAD southern roots and this recipe comes from her childhood. It was always very popular on the brunch table. We've updated her recipe for contemporary vegan palettes.

Cook the peas, drain and rinse under cool water. Place in a bowl and set aside.

Place the tofu, vinegar, lemon juice, mustard, salt and pepper in a food processor and process until smooth. Pour over the peas and mix until the peas are coated. Fold in the red onions.

Serve on a bed of red leaf lettuce.

TOFU BENEDICT WITH HOLLANDAISE SAUCE

Makes 5 servings

1 14 oz. package tofu

Black salt (kala namak)

5 slices English Muffin Bread

10 slices of Tofu Bacon

Hollandaise Sauce

1/2 stick vegan butter,
at room temperature

1 cup silken tofu

1 tablespoon
nutritional yeast

1/2 teaspoon black salt
(use regular sea salt if you
do not have black salt)

1/2 teaspoon turmeric

1/4 teaspoon mustard
powder

2 1/3 tablespoons fresh
lemon juice

2 teaspoons apple
cider vinegar

I STARTED SERVING this at our Mother's Day brunch for one simple reason. It was what I wanted to have on Mother's Day!

Preheat the oven to 400F. Line a baking sheet with parchment.

Slice the tofu into 10 equal slices and place it on the baking sheet. Sprinkle black salt over the top and bake for 20 to 25 minutes.

While the tofu is baking, make the Hollandaise sauce.

Add all ingredients into the food processor. Mix until smooth.

To assemble, toast the English muffin bread. Top with two slices of baked tofu, two slices of tofu bacon in the opposite direction, and a generous portion of hollandaise sauce.

Tofu Benedict with Hollandaise Sauce

Cheesesteak and Peppersteak
Sandwiches, page 45

Chapter 3

LUNCH AT THE CAFÉ

Do you miss lunch at the café? In this section, you will find the recipes for your favorites, including soups, salads, sandwiches, wraps, burgers and paninis. Never had a chance to stop by our café? Now you can try a Rachael sandwich at home and see what all the fuss is about.

SPICY BLACK BEAN SOUP

Makes 8 servings

1 small onion, diced

1 red pepper, diced

1 stalk celery, diced

3 cloves garlic, minced

3 cups black beans

4 cups veggie broth

1 teaspoon cumin

1 tablespoon green chilis, diced

1/2 teaspoon liquid smoke, optional

SOUP IS A staple in our house and a was a big seller at the café. It's easy comfort food and you can leave it simmering on the stove until you are ready to sit down and eat.

Heat the oil in a Dutch oven.

Add the onions, peppers, and celery, and cook over medium heat for about 3 minutes. Add the garlic and cook another 2 minutes. Stir often so the garlic doesn't burn.

Add the black beans, broth, cumin and chilis. Simmer for 3 hours.

Add the liquid smoke, if using, and simmer for another 30 minutes.

CHOWDER

Makes 8 to 10 servings

1 tablespoon olive oil

1 stalk celery, diced

1 shallot, thinly sliced

1 leek, white bulb only, diced

1 clove garlic, minced

2 cups shiitake mushrooms, sliced

3 large potatoes, diced

6 cups vegetable broth

I LOVE THE texture of the shiitake mushrooms in this chowder. They have a nice chewy texture and don't break down like other mushrooms do.

Heat the oil in a Dutch oven.

Add the celery, shallots, and leeks, and cook for 3 to 5 minutes. Add the garlic and mushrooms and cook for another 2 minutes, stirring occasionally so that the garlic doesn't burn.

Add the potatoes and broth. Simmer for 2 to 3 hours.

ONION SOUP

Makes 6 to 8 servings

2 tablespoons olive oil

3 large onions, thinly sliced

2 shallots, thinly sliced

1/4 cup white wine, optional

5 cups vegetable broth

1/2 teaspoon thyme

Croutons

2 slices of sourdough or other crusty bread

THIS SIMPLE SOUP is an all-time favorite of mine. Be patient when making it, because the longer and slower the onions cook, the better the soup will be.

In a large pot or Dutch oven, heat the oil over medium to low heat.

Add the onions and shallots. Cook for 1 to 2 hours on low heat-stirring occasionally, until the onions start to caramelize and are golden in color. The longer and slower you cook the onions, the better they will be.

While the onions are cooking, make the croutons. Preheat the oven to 250F and line a baking sheet with parchment paper. Cut the bread into quarters and place on the baking sheet. Bake for 30 to 40 minutes, until the bread is toasted.

Now, back to the soup. Stir in the wine, if using. Add the broth and thyme, and let the soup simmer for 1 hour.

To assemble, place a slice of bread/crouton in the bottom of a soup bowl. Add 2 tablespoons of vegan cheese and top with soup. Serve immediately.

CAFÉ TIP
Just before serving this soup, srinkle in a 1/2 cup of vegan cheese.

MINESTRONE

Makes 8 to 10 servings

1 tablespoon olive oil

2 carrots, diced

1 green pepper, diced

1 small onion, diced

1 stalk celery, diced

2 cloves garlic, minced

3 cups diced tomatoes

4 cups vegetable broth

1 teaspoon basil

1 teaspoon thyme

1 cup cannellini beans

1/2 cup uncooked
elbow pasta

1 cup cabbage, thinly sliced

MY MOM ALWAYS said this was a good soup to make when you have leftover vegetables and pasta. As a result, the soup is a little different every time you make it.

Heat the oil in a Dutch oven.

Add the carrots, peppers, onions, and celery and sauté for 3 to 4 minutes. Add the garlic and cook for 1 minute, being careful not to burn the garlic. Add the tomatoes, broth, basil, thyme and beans.

Simmer for 2 hours. Add the pasta and simmer for 30 more minutes, until the pasta is al dente. Stir in the cabbage just before you are ready to serve.

LENTIL SOUP

Makes 6 servings

2 tablespoons olive oil

1 stalk celery, diced

1 small onion, diced

3 carrots, diced

3 tomatoes, diced

1 cup uncooked lentils

1/4 cup fresh parsley

1 1/2 teaspoons tarragon

1 1/2 teaspoons thyme

1 teaspoon black pepper

6 cups vegetable broth

THE FIRST TIME I ever tasted lentils was when my mother-in-law made this soup. I was very skeptical, but wanted to be polite, so I ate it. Who knew that lentils were so tasty? Thanks, Mom.

In a large soup pot, heat the oil and sauté the celery, onion, and carrots until soft, about 5 minutes.

Add the tomatoes, lentils, parsley, spices, and broth, and simmer for about one hour or until lentils are cooked through.

Lentil Soup

MUSHROOM SOUP

Makes 6 to 8 servings

2 tablespoons olive oil

1 small onion, diced

1 stalk celery, diced

1 clove garlic, minced

1 cup white button mushrooms, sliced

1 cup baby bella mushrooms, sliced

1 cup shiitake mushrooms, sliced

1/4 cup white wine, optional

5 cups vegetable broth

THIS MUSHROOM SOUP is delicious no matter what kind of mushrooms you use. Do you only like white button mushrooms? Delicious. But, for a mushroom lover like me, the flavor and texture is even better when you use three or more different kinds. Experiment with your favorites and create your own version of this soup.

In a large pan, add the oil, onions, celery, and garlic, and sauté over medium heat for 3 to 5 minutes.

Add mushrooms and cook for another 5 to 8 minutes until the mushrooms have softened and are lightly browned.

Stir in the wine, if using, and add the broth. Simmer on low for one hour, stirring occasionally.

BROCCOLI SOUP

Makes 8 to 10 servings

2 tablespoons olive oil

1 small onion, diced

1 stalk celery, diced

1 shallot, diced

2 cloves garlic, minced

3 cups chopped broccoli

2 medium sized potatoes, quartered

3 tablespoons nutritional yeast

1/2 teaspoon Dijon mustard

6 cups vegetable broth

Heat the oil over medium heat in a Dutch oven.

Add the onions, celery, and shallots and cook for 4 minutes. Add the garlic and cook for another minute, being careful not to burn the garlic.

Stir in the broccoli, potatoes, nutritional yeast, Dijon mustard and broth. Stir well and simmer for 2 hours

CHILI

Makes 8 servings

2 tablespoons olive oil

2 stalks celery, diced

1 large onion, diced

3 carrots, diced

1 red pepper, diced

1 green pepper, diced

3 cloves garlic, minced

1 cup kidney beans

1 cup black beans

1 cup pinto beans

4 cups diced tomatoes

1 cup frozen corn

1 teaspoon chili powder

1 teaspoon cumin

1 teaspoon oregano

THIS RECIPE CALLS for three cups of beans. We have listed the ones we like, but be creative and use whatever you have on hand. Our version is very mild, but spice it up by adding jalapeño peppers or hot sauce.

Heat the oil in a Dutch oven.

Add the celery, onions, carrots, and peppers and sauté for 3 to 5 minutes. Add the garlic and cook for another minute, stirring to keep the garlic from burning. Add the beans, tomatoes, corn, and spices.

Simmer for 4 hours.

BARLEY SALAD

Makes 2 to 4 servings

1 cup barley

3 tablespoons balsamic vinegar

3 tablespoons olive oil

2 tablespoons maple syrup

1/2 teaspoon sea salt

1 red pepper, diced

1 cup chopped green onion

1 cup cherry tomatoes, sliced in half

Place the barley in a saucepan with 3 cups of water. Bring to a boil, turn the heat down, cover and cook for 30 minutes. Remove from heat, drain and rinse under cool water. Add to a mixing bowl.

In a small bowl, mix together the balsamic vinegar, oil, maple syrup, and sea salt. Pour over the cooled barley. Gently stir in the red pepper and green onions.

Top with cherry tomatoes, cover, and refrigerate for 30 minutes before serving.

Potato Salad

POTATO SALAD

Makes 6 to 8 servings

5 Yukon gold or red potatoes, peeled

1/2 cup diced sweet onion

1 cup vegan mayo

1 tablespoon apple cider vinegar

1 teaspoon Dijon mustard

Salt & pepper, to taste

1/4 cup chopped parsley

MAYBE IT'S MY Irish roots, but there are few things I like better than potato salad on a hot summer day.

Boil potatoes in water until cooked, but still firm. Drain and cool. When cooled, cut into bite-sized pieces, and place in a large bowl. Add the onions to the potatoes.

In a small bowl, mix together the mayo, vinegar, and mustard. Whisk until smooth.

Add to the potatoes and gently mix together. Add salt and pepper, to taste. When ready to serve, top with freshly chopped parsley.

COUSCOUS SALAD

Makes 5 to 6 servings

Couscous

2 cups vegetable broth

1 1/3 cup pearl couscous

Dressing

2 cloves roasted garlic

2 1/2 tablespoons olive oil

2 tablespoons balsamic vinegar

1 teaspoon fresh lemon juice

1/2 teaspoon sea salt

Salad

1 red pepper, chopped

1/2 sweet onion, diced

1 cup frozen, canned, or fresh corn kernels

1 cup black beans

1/4 cup chopped parsley

Bring the broth to a boil. Stir in the couscous and simmer for 1 minute. Remove from heat, cover and let sit for 5 minutes.

Make the dressing. In a small bowl, whisk together the roasted garlic, oil, vinegar, lemon juice, and salt.

To assemble the salad, add the couscous, red pepper, onions, corn, and black beans to a big bowl. Pour the dressing over the salad and toss to combine. Top with chopped parsley.

Refrigerate for one hour before serving.

TOFISHY

Makes 3 sandwiches

Tartar Sauce

1/2 cup vegan mayo

1/4 cup chopped sweet pickle

Pinch of onion powder

Tofishy

1 14 oz. package extra firm tofu

2 tablespoons corn starch

1/2 cup corn meal

1/2 teaspoon onion powder

1/4 teaspoon sea salt

2 tablespoons olive oil, for frying

3 sandwich rolls, toasted

Toppings

Lettuce

Tomato slices

Onion slices

Mix all of the sauce ingredients together and set aside.

Cut tofu into 9 equal slices, approximately 1/2-inch thick. Place on paper towels for 5 to 10 minutes to dry off excess moisture.

Combine corn starch, corn meal, onion powder, and salt in a small mixing bowl. Dip each piece of tofu into the corn meal mixture. Heat the oil in a skillet and fry for 3 to 5 minutes per side.

To assemble, spread 2 tablespoons of tartar sauce on each side of the roll. Add 2 to 3 slices of tofu and top with lettuce, tomatoes, and onions.

CHEESESTEAK

Makes 2

Teriyaki Sauce

1 tablespoon olive oil

2 tablespoons brown sugar

2 tablespoons tamari

1/2 teaspoon garlic powder

Steak

1 tablespoon olive oil

1 1/2 cup thinly sliced seitan cutlets, recipe on page 15

1/2 cup thinly sliced onion

Teriyaki sauce

1/2 cup Daiya cheese

2 12" wraps, or your favorite roll

WE ALWAYS LOVED it when we could make believers out of our non-vegan customers, some of whom were "dragged" to the café by their vegan family members. This is one of the items that made them want to come back and try more things.

Add all of the sauce ingredients to a small bowl. Mix well and set aside.

Heat the oil in a large skillet. Add the seitan and onions and cook for 3 to 5 minutes, until the onions are soft. Add the teriyaki sauce and cook for another 3 to 4 minutes. Turn off the heat and stir in the Daiya cheese. When the cheese is melted, divide mixture in half and place in the rolls.

PEPPERSTEAK

Makes 2

Pepper Sauce

1 tablespoon olive oil

2 tablespoons brown sugar

2 tablespoons tamari

1 clove garlic, minced

1/8 teaspoon red pepper flakes

Steak

1 tablespoon olive oil

1 1/2 cups sliced seitan, cut into strips about the size of French fries

1/2 onion, sliced

1/2 red pepper, cut into strips

1/2 green pepper, cut into strips

THIS IS A spicier version of our beloved cheesesteak.

Mix together sauce ingredients and set aside.

Heat the oil in a skillet. Add the seitan, onions, and peppers. Cook for 3 to 5 minutes until the onions are soft.

Add the pepper sauce and cook for another 3 to 4 minutes.

Divide in half and serve on your favorite wraps or rolls.

See a photo of Cheesesteak and Peppersteak sandwiches on page 32.

THE RACHAEL

Makes 2 sandwiches, with extra coleslaw to serve on the side

Rachael Sauce

1/2 cup vegan mayo

2 tablespoons tomato paste

2 tablespoons chopped sweet pickles

Coleslaw

1/2 head green cabbage

1 carrot

About 1 tablespoon fresh lemon juice

3 tablespoons sugar

1/4 cup vegan mayo

Salt & pepper, to taste

To Assemble

4 slices seitan

1 tablespoon olive oil

4 slices rye bread

2 tablespoons vegan butter

Coleslaw

Rachael sauce

THIS SANDWICH WAS by far the most popular item on the menu at the café, and our most requested recipe. There are several elements to building this sandwich, but taking the time to make everything you will need is definitely worth the effort.

To make the Rachael sauce, mix all of the ingredients together in a small bowl. Set aside.

Using a food processor fitted with the grater attachment, make the coleslaw by shredding the cabbage and carrots. Add to a large bowl. Juice the lemon over the cabbage and carrots, and add the sugar and mayo. Season with salt and pepper.

Mix well and let sit for 5 to 10 minutes.

Fry the seitan slices in the oil for 3 to 4 minutes per side, until golden brown. Remove from the skillet and set aside.

Butter the rye bread, and cook, butter side down, in the same skillet for about 4 minutes, until lightly browned.

Spread the Rachael sauce on a slice of rye bread. Add 2 slices of seitan, a third of a cup of coleslaw, and top with extra Rachael sauce. Top with the other slice of rye bread and enjoy!

The Rachael

GRILLED SEITAN WRAP

Serves 2

Smokey Garlic Aioli

1/4 cup vegan mayo

1 small clove garlic, minced

1 teaspoon mustard

1 drop liquid smoke, optional

The Wrap

1 tablespoon olive oil

3 slices of seitan, cut into strips

Smokey Garlic Aioli

2 wraps

Toppings

Lettuce

Tomato slices

Onion slices

THIS WAS OUR most popular wrap at the café. As we like to say, "It's all about the sauce," because it's smoky and garlicky and delicious. Be careful, though, don't use too much liquid smoke, as it can be overwhelming.

Mix all of the aioli ingredients together and set aside.

Heat the oil in a large skillet. Add the seitan slices and cook for about 5 minutes, until lightly browned. Spread aioli on the wrap, add half of the seitan, and top with lettuce, tomatoes, and onions.

TERIYAKI SEITAN WRAP

Serves 2

Ingredients for Grilled Seitan Wrap, above

Teriyaki Sauce

1 Tablespoon olive oil

2 Tablespoon brown sugar

2 Tablespoon tamari

1/2 teaspoon garlic powder

THIS VARIATION OF the Grilled Seitan Wrap is great for those who like the salty sweetness of teriyaki instead of a garlicky aioli.

Mix all of the Teriyaki Sauce ingredients together.

Follow the instructions for the Grilled Seitan Wrap, but cook the seitan in 2 tablespoons of Teriyaki Sauce instead of oil.

Eggless Egg Salad Wrap

Serves 4

1 package firm tofu

1/2 teaspoon turmeric

1/2 teaspoon Dijon mustard

1/4 teaspoon salt

1/4 teaspoon garlic powder

1/4 cup vegan mayo

1/2 cup sweet pickles, chopped

1/4 cup diced celery

Add-ins

Lettuce

Tomato

Shredded carrots

Sliced onions

Cucumber slices

Preheat the oven to 350F.

In a mixing bowl, crumble the tofu and mix with the turmeric, Dijon mustard, salt, and garlic powder. Spread onto a baking sheet and bake for 20 minutes.

Let cool. Place the baked tofu into clean bowl and add the mayo, pickles, and celery. Mix well.

To assemble, place one cup of the mixture onto a wrap. Top with lettuce, tomato, carrots, onion, and cucumbers. Fold in the sides, roll up, and enjoy

Corn & Black Bean Salsa

Makes 4 cups of salsa

1 cup corn

2 cup black beans

1 red pepper, diced

1 medium sweet onion, diced

1/4 cup chopped cilantro

1/4 cup olive oil

1/4 cup balsamic vinegar

1/2 teaspoon cumin

Salt and pepper to taste

Place the corn, black beans, pepper and onion in a bowl.

Whisk together the olive oil, balsamic vinegar, cumin, salt and pepper, and add to the bowl. Mix together, add the cilantro and refrigerate for 30 minutes.

Serve with corn chips.

See a photo of Corn & Black Bean Salsa on page 7.

Spinach & Soysage Quesadilla/Burrito

Serves 2 to 3

1/2 cup diced onion

1 cup Soysage mix, recipe on page 20

1 cup chopped spinach

1 cup vegan cream cheese

2 to 3 wraps

THESE WERE AS popular at breakfast and brunch as they were at lunch.

Heat 1 tablespoon of oil in a skillet. Add the onions and Soysage mix and cook for 4 to 5 minutes. Remove the pan from the heat and mix in the spinach.

Transfer the mixture to a bowl, and add the cream cheese. Mix well.

To assemble a burrito, place one cup of the mixture onto a wrap. Fold in the sides, roll up, and pan fry until lightly browned on all sides.

To make the quesadilla, place one cup of the mixture onto a wrap. Fold in half and pan fry until lightly browned on each side.

Aila Burrito

Serves 4

1 14 oz. package firm tofu, cubed

1 cup cooked black beans

1/4 teaspoon salt

1/4 teaspoon cumin

1/4 cup water

Assembly

1 cup cooked rice

1 cup vegan cheese

Hot sauce

4 flour tortillas

Accompaniments

Salsa

Vegan sour cream

ONE DAY WHEN our granddaughter, Aila, was visiting the café, she asked for the Spinach and Soysage Burrito, without the spinach and Soysage. She asked if we could put baked tofu, rice, and spicy beans on it instead. And of course, some vegan cheese. It turned out to be a tasty creation, so we added it to the menu.

Preheat the oven to 350F. Place the tofu on a baking sheet and bake for 20 minutes.

While tofu is cooking, add the beans, salt, cumin and water to a sauce pan. Cook over medium heat for 10 minutes, stirring occasionally to keep the beans from burning.

To assemble, place one-fourth of the tofu, one-fourth of the beans and a quarter of a cup rice on each tortilla. Top with a quarter cup of cheese, and a splash of hot sauce. Roll up, carefully tucking in the sides as you go, and fry until all sides are lightly browned.

Serve with salsa and sour cream.

Spinach & Soysage
Quesadillas

Black Bean Veggie Burger

Serves 4 to 6

2 cups cooked black beans

1 cup cooked rice

1/2 green pepper, chopped

1/2 small red onion, chopped

1/2 cup fresh or frozen corn kernels

1 carrot, shredded

1 cup fresh bread crumbs

Garlic Aioli

1/2 cup vegan mayo

1 clove garlic, minced

FOR A GLUTEN-FREE burger, use mashed sweet potatoes in place of the bread crumbs

Place the black beans in a large bowl and, using a potato masher or the back of a spoon, mash at least half of the beans, leaving some whole, for texture. Add the remaining ingredients and mix together until combined.

Using 3/4 cup of mixture per burger, form into patties and fry in a tablespoon of oil until browned on both sides. Serve with Garlic Aioli.

To make the aioli, mix the mayo and garlic together.

Black Bean Veggie Burger Panini

Ingredients for Black Bean Veggie Burgers and Garlic Aioli, above

1 teaspoon Sriracha hot sauce

THIS IS ANOTHER way we served our black bean burger at the café. And, as it turns out, was our most popular panini. Because, who doesn't love a veggie burger with hot sauce and cheese added?

Make the garlic aioli and add the Sriracha. Spread the aioli on a wrap or bun. Add a cooked black bean veggie burger, top with some arugula, and your favorite vegan cheese.

Cook in a panini grill until cheese melts, 4 to 5 minutes.

AMERICAN BURGER

Makes 6 to 8

2 1/2 cups textured vegetable protein (TVP)

1/2 cup oats

2 cups boiling water

2 tablespoons tomato paste

2 teaspoons Dijon mustard

2 teaspoons tahini

1 teaspoons olive oil

1 tablespoon nutritional yeast

1 teaspoon onion powder

1 teaspoon garlic powder

2 teaspoons tamari

2 cups bread crumbs

Toppings

Lettuce

Tomatoes

Onions

Ketchup

Mustard

In a large mixing bowl, add TVP, oats, and water. Stir and let sit for 1 hour. Add remaining ingredients and mix well.

Using 3/4 cup of mixture per burger, form into patties pan fry in 2 tablespoons of oil. Serve on a bun topped with lettuce, tomatoes, onions, ketchup, and mustard.

LENTIL BURGER

Serves 4

1 cup cooked lentils

2 1/2 tablespoons tamari

1 1/2 tablespoons ketchup

2 cups wheat-free seitan crumbles

1/2 cup finely chopped onion

Garlic Aioli

1/2 cup vegan mayo

1 clove garlic, minced

Place the lentils, tamari and ketchup in a food processor and process until smooth.

Add the seitan crumbles and pulse until the crumbles are mixed in but not completely pureed. Transfer mixture to a bowl and add onions.

Using 3/4 cup of mixture per burger, form into patties and pan fry until nicely browned on both sides. Serve with Garlic Aioli.

To make the aioli, mix the mayo and garlic together.

Veggie Cakes,
page 55

CHICK PEA CUTLETS

Serves 4

Cutlets

3 cups chickpeas

1 teaspoon paprika

1/2 teaspoon cumin

1 tablespoon fresh lemon juice

1 tablespoon tamari

1 tablespoon vegetable broth paste

2 tablespoons olive oil

1 clove garlic, minced

1 cup panko crumbs

Sauce

1/2 cup reserved chickpea mixture

1 tablespoon olive oil

1 teaspoon lemon juice

1 tablespoon tahini

1/2 teaspoon cumin

Place chickpeas in the bowl of a food processor and process on low until the chickpeas start to break up. Add the paprika, cumin, lemon juice, tamari, broth paste, oil, and garlic, and mix well.

Take out half of a cup of the mixture and set aside before adding the panko crumbs. Mix the panko crumbs thoroughly into the chickpea mixture.

Preheat the oven to 350F.

Using one cup of mix per cutlet, form into cutlets and bake 30 to 40 minutes. While the cutlets are cooking, prepare the sauce.

To make the sauce, mix the ingredients together.

No Chicken Salad Wrap

Serves 3

3 seitan cutlets

Oil, for frying

Sauce

1/2 cup vegan mayo

1/2 teaspoon vegan chicken broth paste

Assembly

1/3 cup diced celery

Lettuce, Tomato, Onion

3 rolls

Slice the seitan cutlets in half and pan fry in a teaspoon oil until lightly browned of both sides. Remove from the pan and set aside to cool.

Make the sauce by mixing together the mayo and broth paste.

Chop the cutlets into bite sized pieces, and add to the bowl of sauce. Add the celery and mix well.

Serve with lettuce, tomatoes, and onions on a roll.

Cabbage & Ginger Dumplings

Makes 30 to 40 dumplings

1 head cabbage, shredded

1 teaspoon salt

1 clove garlic, minced

2 tablespoons freshly grated ginger

Hot water

2 tablespoons olive oil

1/4 teaspoon turmeric

1 teaspoon cumin

Dumpling wrappers

WHEN A COUPLE of our friends made these one weekend, we were all instantly in love. We decided to make a few and see how people responded at the café. We couldn't keep up with the demand after that.

Add shredded cabbage, salt, garlic, and ginger to large mixing bowl. Pour enough hot water over the cabbage to cover it completely. Let sit for 5 minutes. Drain the water and squeeze out any excess water from cabbage mixture.

Stir in the oil, turmeric, and cumin.

Place 2 teaspoons of the mixture onto the center of a dumpling wrapper. Moisten the edges of the wrapper with water and pinch the edges together.

Oil your steamer basket and place the dumplings in the steamer, ensuring they are not touching. Cover and steam for 10 to 12 minutes.

Veggie Cakes

Serves 4 to 6

Cakes

1/2 red pepper, diced

1/2 green pepper, diced

1/2 medium onion, diced

3 stalks celery, diced

1 14 oz. package firm tofu

1/2 cup vegan mayo

2 1/2 teaspoons Old Bay seasoning

2 1/2 cup fresh bread crumbs

Oil for frying

Mustard Sauce

2 tablespoons vegan mayo

1 tablespoon Dijon mustard

Hot Sauce

2 tablespoons vegan mayo

2 teaspoons hot sauce

Tartar Sauce

2 tablespoons vegan mayo

1 tablespoon sweet pickles, finely chopped

1/4 teaspoon onion powder

Add red pepper, green pepper, onions, and celery to the food processor and pulse until minced.

Heat oil in a frying pan over medium heat, add the vegetables, and cook over medium heat until softened. Transfer to a mixing bowl

Drain the tofu, add to the food processor, and puree until smooth. Add to the vegetables, along with the mayo, Old Bay, and bread crumbs.

Using a 3/4 cup measure, form into patties, and fry, using a small amount of oil, over medium heat, until browned on both sides. Serve with the any, or all, of the sauces below.

To make any of the sauces, mix all of the ingredients together.

Faux Turkey Dinner,
page 19

Chapter 4

MAIN DISHES

There are times when you want something more sub-
stantial than a sandwich or a wrap. In this section, we offer
a few recipes for the main dishes we served at the café. If
you wish, you can make these in advance and save them
for another time because they freeze and keep well.

LASAGNA

Makes 10 servings

Spinach Ricotta

2 14 oz. packages tofu

2 cloves garlic

1 tablespoon olive oil

1 tablespoon nutritional yeast

1 teaspoon salt

1 cup fresh chopped spinach

Lasagna

12 uncooked lasagna noodles

1/2 onion, sliced

1 zucchini, sliced

1 yellow summer squash, sliced

1 green pepper, sliced

1 red pepper, sliced

Spinach ricotta

2 cups tomato sauce

2 cups diced tomatoes

2 cups Daiya cheese

To make ricotta, add all ingredients to a food processor and pulse until crumbly. Set aside.

Cook the lasagna noodles according to the package directions. Set aside.

Prepare the vegetables and mix together in a bowl.

To assemble the lasagna, add half a cup of tomato sauce and half a cup diced tomatoes into the bottom of a lasagna pan. Place 4 noodles on top of the tomatoes. Spread half of the ricotta over the noodles. Top with half of the onion, zucchini, summer squash, and peppers. Pour half of a cup of tomato sauce and half a cup diced tomatoes over the vegetables. Repeat this process for the next layer. Top with the last 4 noodles and the remaining sauce and tomatoes. Sprinkle the Daiya over the top.

Cover and bake at 350F for 45 to 50 minutes.

CAFÉ TIP

If you are using uncooked noodles, you will need to cook for an extra 15 to 30 minutes.

TOFU POT PIE

Makes 8 servings

1 14 oz. package firm tofu

2 tablespoons vegan butter

2 tablespoons flour

2 cups vegetable broth

1 cup peas

2 large Yukon gold potatoes, peeled, and diced

1 carrot, peeled and sliced

Pie crust for top and bottom, recipe on page 82

Preheat the oven to 350F. Line a baking sheet with parchment paper.

Cut the tofu into cubes and place on the baking sheet. Bake for 15 minutes. When the tofu is ready, take out of the oven and set aside. Leave the oven on.

While the tofu is cooking, make the gravy. In a saucepan, melt the butter. Add the flour and whisk until crumbly. Slowly stir in the broth, whisking constantly to avoid lumps. Bring to a boil, remove from heat and whisk for another minute. Set aside.

To assemble, line the bottom of the pie plate with one of the pie crusts. Add the tofu, peas, potatoes and carrot into the crust and pour the sauce over the top. Top with the second pie crust. Using a sharp knife, cut two slits into the top of the crust.

Bake on a cookie sheet for one hour.

MAC & CHEESE

Makes 8 servings

1 cup Basic Cheese Sauce, recipe on page 17

1 lb. rotini or mini-shell pasta

Cook the pasta according to the package directions. Rinse and set aside while you make the cheese sauce.

Once it is completed, place the pasta in a large bowl, stir in the cheese sauce and serve.

Quinoa Casserole

QUINOA CASSEROLE

Makes 6 to 8 servings

1/2 cup uncooked quinoa

1 cup water

1 zucchini, diced

1 yellow squash, diced

1 onion, diced

4 cups chopped tomatoes

2 cloves garlic, minced

1 cup Daiya cheese, optional

Preheat the oven to 350F.

Place the quinoa in a fine mesh strainer. Rinse the quinoa until the water runs clear. Add the quinoa and water to saucepan and simmer for 15 minutes.

While the quinoa is cooking, dice the zucchini, summer squash, and onion. Add to a large mixing bowl.

When the quinoa is cooked, add it the vegetables along with the tomatoes. Add the minced garlic and gently stir everything together. Transfer to a baking dish. Top with cheese, if using, and bake for 30 to 45 minutes

QUICHE

Makes 6 to 8 servings

1 14 oz. package firm tofu

1 lb. package silken tofu

1/2 teaspoon turmeric

1/2 teaspoon salt

1/2 teaspoon garlic powder

2 tablespoons nutri. yeast

1/2 cup diced onion

1 cup Soysage Mix, recipe on page 20

1 cup Daiya cheese

Pie crust, optional, recipe on page 82

WE OFTEN MAKE this without the pie crust. Try it both ways and see what you think.

Preheat the oven to 350F.

In a large mixing bowl, crumble the tofus. Add the remaining ingredients and mix together. Place mixture in a pie plate, with or without the crust, and bake for one hour.

SPINACH & MUSHROOM QUICHE

Makes 6 to 8 servings

Ingredients for Quiche above, omitting Soysage mix

1 cup spinach, chopped

1 cup mushrooms, sliced

To make this variation, replace the Soysage mix with a cup each chopped spinach and sliced mushrooms. Sauté for 3 minutes and add to the quiche recipe. Bake as directed above.

Chapter 5

CAFÉ BREADS

A good, crusty bread goes well with just about any main dish, and sliced bread or rolls are essential ingredients for any successful sandwich or burger. At the café, we made a variety of breads, sandwich rolls, muffins and coffee cakes, perfect for breakfast, lunch or dinner.

WHITE SANDWICH ROLLS

Makes 12 rolls

2 teaspoons yeast

1 tablespoon sugar

1/2 cup warm water

2 1/2 cups all-purpose flour

1/3 cup soy milk

1 teaspoon salt

2 tablespoons vegan butter

WE ALWAYS MADE our own sandwich and burger rolls at the café. They are easy to make! You can cut the recipe in half and use a smaller pan if you want to make a smaller batch. We recommend using a cookie sheet that has sides to make the rolls.

Preheat the oven to 350F. Grease a rimmed baking sheet and set aside.

Add the yeast, sugar, and water to the bowl of your stand mixer and let sit for 15 minutes.

Add the flour, soy milk, salt, and butter. Using the dough hook attachment, mix on low for 10 minutes. Let rest for 20 minutes, and then mix on low for 5 minutes.

Press dough evenly onto the baking sheet. Gently cut the dough, using a sharp knife, into 12 equal parts to make12 rolls. This will make it easier to separate the rolls after they are baked.

Cover and let the dough rise for one hour. Bake for 20 minutes.

WHEAT SANDWICH ROLLS

Makes 12 rolls

1 tablespoon yeast

3/4 cup warm water

1 tablespoon molasses

1 cup whole wheat flour

1 1/2 cups white flour

1/3 cup soy milk

1 teaspoon salt

1 tablespoon vegan butter

Preheat the oven to 350F. Grease a rimmed baking sheet and set aside.

Add the yeast, water and molasses to the bowl of your stand mixer and let sit for 15 minutes.

Add the flours, soy milk, salt, and butter. Using the dough hook attachment, mix on low for 10 minutes. Let rest for 20 minutes, and then mix on low for 5 minutes.

Press dough put evenly onto the baking sheet. Gently cut the dough, using a sharp knife, into 12 equal parts to make 12 rolls. This will make it easier to separate the rolls after they are baked.

Cover and let the dough rise for one hour. Bake for 20 minutes.

ENGLISH MUFFIN BREAD

Makes 1 loaf

2 1/2 teaspoons yeast

1 teaspoon sugar

1/2 cup warm water

3 cups flour

1 teaspoon salt

1/4 teaspoon baking soda

1/2 cup soy milk

Vegan butter or oil, for greasing the bread pan

1 tablespoon corn meal, for dusting the bread pan

I FOUND THIS recipe one day when I was going through an old family recipe box. I love English muffins so I decided to try it. I was instantly in love.

Prepare your loaf pan by greasing the bottom and sides with butter or oil. Sprinkle the corn meal on the bottom of the pan and set aside.

Add the yeast, sugar, and warm water to bowl of your stand mixer. Stir gently and let sit for 10 minutes. Add the flour, salt, baking soda, and soy milk. Using the dough hook attachment, mix for 10 minutes. Let rest for 20 minutes. Mix on low for 5 minutes. Remove the dough from the bowl and roll into a loaf. Transfer to your bread pan and gently press into the pan, ensuring the bread fills the pan, and cover.

Preheat the oven to 400F.

Let the dough rise for 90 minutes. Bake for 18 to 20 minutes.

Let the bread cool for 10 minutes before removing it from the pan.

OATMEAL BREAD

Makes 1 loaf

2 teaspoons yeast

1/4 cup brown sugar

3/4 cup warm water

1/2 cup soy milk

3 1/2 cups flour

1 cup oats

1 teaspoon salt

2 tablespoons canola oil

Butter or oil, for greasing the bread pan

Prepare your loaf pan by greasing the bottom and sides with butter or oil.

Add the yeast, brown sugar, water, and soy milk to the bowl of your stand mixer. Stir gently and let sit for 10 minutes. Add the flour, oatmeal, salt, and canola oil. Using the dough hook attachment, mix for 10 minutes. Let rest for 20 minutes. Mix on low for five minutes. Press the dough into the prepared bread pan, ensuring the bread fills the pan, and cover.

Cover and let rise for one hour.

Preheat the oven to 350F. Bake for 35 minutes.

Skillet Corn Bread

Makes 8 to 10 servings

1 1/4 cup flour

3/4 cup corn meal

1/2 cup sugar

2 teaspoons baking powder

1 cup soy milk

5 tablespoons vegan butter

I LOVE CORN BREAD made in a cast iron skillet. If you don't have a cast iron, you can make it in a 9" cake pan.

Preheat the oven to 400F.

Put butter in cast iron skillet and place in the oven until melted. Remove from oven and set aside.

Mix together the dry ingredients. Add soy milk and melted butter. Mix until dry ingredients are moistened. Do not overmix.

Bake for 25 minutes.

Herb & Garlic Corn Bread

Makes 8 to 10 servings

Ingredients for Skillet Corn Bread, above

Herb and Garlic Butter

5 tablespoons vegan butter, softened

3 teaspoons fresh chives, finely chopped

1/2 teaspoon fresh dill, finely chopped

2 teaspoons fresh parsley, finely chopped

1/4 teaspoon onion powder

1/2 clove of garlic, minced

FOLLOW THE RECIPE for corn bread, above, but substitute this decadent herb and garlic butter for the original's plain butter.

To make the herb and garlic butter, combine ingredients in a small bowl. Mix well.

Skillet
Corn Bread

ORANGE RAISIN BREAD
Makes 1 loaf

2 cups flour

1 teaspoon baking powder

1/2 teaspoon baking soda

1/2 cup sugar

1 1/4 cup orange juice

2 tablespoons vegan butter, at room temperature

1 teaspoon vanilla

1 cup raisins

Preheat the oven to 350F. Grease a loaf pan and set aside.

Place all ingredients into the bowl of a stand mixer fitted with a paddle attachment. Mix on medium for 3 to 4 minutes. Pour the batter into the loaf pan and bake for 45 to 50 minutes.

BANANA BREAD
Makes 1 loaf

2 cups flour

1/2 teaspoon baking soda

1 teaspoon baking powder

1/4 teaspoon cinnamon

1/2 teaspoon salt

1/2 cup vegan butter, at room temperature

1 cup sugar

3 coarsely mashed very ripe bananas

1/3 cup soy milk

1 teaspoon vanilla

Preheat the oven to 350F.

Mix the first 5 ingredients, the flour through salt, in a bowl and set aside.

To a separate bowl, add the butter and sugar and cream together using a hand mixer until smooth. Add the mashed bananas, soy milk and vanilla. Slowly add the flour mixture, and mix by hand, until smooth.

Bake for one hour, or until a skewer comes out clean.

BLUEBERRY COFFEE CAKE

Makes 8 to 10 servings

2 cups flour

1/2 cup sugar

1 teaspoon baking powder

1/2 teaspoon baking soda

1/2 teaspoon salt

1/4 cup vegan butter

1 1/3 cups soy milk

1 teaspoon vanilla

1 1/2 cups blueberries

Preheat the oven to 375F. Grease and flour an 8" x 8" pan.

Combine the flour, sugar, baking powder, baking soda, and salt to a large mixing bowl. Add the butter, soy milk, and vanilla and stir until everything is mixed in. It's okay for the batter to be a little lumpy. Carefully stir in the blueberries.

Bake for 30 to 40 minutes

LEMON BLUEBERRY MUFFINS

Makes 12 muffins

1 1/4 cups soy milk

1 tablespoon lemon juice

1 teaspoon fresh lemon zest

1/2 teaspoon vanilla

2 cups flour

1/2 cup sugar

1 teaspoon baking powder

1/2 teaspoon baking soda

1/2 teaspoon salt

1/4 cup vegan butter, at room temperature

1 1/2 cups blueberries

2 tablespoons sugar, for the tops of the muffins

Preheat the oven to 400F. Place the muffin cups in the muffin pan and set aside.

Add the soy milk, lemon juice, lemon zest, and vanilla to a small mixing bowl. Stir and set aside.

Mix together the flour, sugar, baking powder, baking soda, salt, and butter. Add the soy milk mixture and stir until everything is mixed in. It's okay for the batter to be a little lumpy. Carefully stir in the blueberries.

Use an ice cream scooper or 1/3 measuring cup to place batter into each muffin cup. Sprinkle sugar over the top of each muffin. Bake for 20 to 25 minutes.

Cinnamon Bread

Cinnamon Bread or Rolls

Makes 1 loaf or 8 rolls

1 cup vanilla soy milk

1/4 cup vegan butter

1/4 cup sugar

1/2 teaspoon salt

3 1/2 cups flour

2 1/2 teaspoon yeast

Filling

1/3 cup brown sugar

2 teaspoons cinnamon

Start by making the filling. Combine the brown sugar and cinnamon in a small bowl and set aside.

Add the vanilla soy milk, butter, sugar, salt, flour, and yeast to the mixing bowl. Mix on low for 8 minutes.

Using your dough hook attachment, mix on low for 8 minutes.

Cover and let the dough rest for 30 minutes. Mix again for another 5 minutes.

To make bread, roll out the dough into an 8" x 10" rectangle. Spread the filling over the dough. Starting at the end of the long side, and roll it into a log. Place in a greased loaf pan with the seam side down.

Allow bread to rise for one hour. Bake at 350F for 35 minutes. Allow to cool for 5 minutes before removing from the loaf pan.

To make rolls, roll the long as described above, and cut into 8 equal pieces. Place the rolls in a greased 9" cake pan. Cover, and allow to rise until doubled in size.

Bake at 350F for 25 to 30 minutes.

Overnight Cinnamon Rolls

Makes 8 rolls

Ingredients for Cinnamon Rolls, above

Make the Cinnamon Rolls the same as above. After placing the cut rolls in the cake pan, cover with plastic wrap and place in the refrigerator to rise overnight. In the morning, remove the rolls from the refrigerator and set on the counter for 30 minutes. Bake at 350F for 25 to 30 minutes.

Ginger Crinkles,
page 74

Chapter 6

THE BAKERY CASE

Do you miss the bakery case as much as we do? Now you can recreate it at home. These cakes, pies and treats were always very popular with our customers at the café, both young and old. Because most of the recipes in this section are easy to make, you have no reason not to indulge!

GINGER CRINKLES

Makes 12 cookies

3/4 cup canola oil

1 cup sugar

1/4 cup water

1/4 cup molasses

2 cups flour

2 teaspoons baking soda

1 teaspoon cinnamon

1 teaspoon ginger

Extra sugar to roll cookies in

IT IS IMPORTANT to make these cookies as soon as the batter is mixed to prevent the oil from separating from the batter.

Preheat the oven to 350F. Line a cookie sheet with parchment paper.

Mix together the oil, sugar, water, and molasses until smooth. Add the remaining ingredients and mix well.

Use a tablespoon measure to form into balls, roll in sugar, and place on the cookie sheet.

Bake for 10 minutes.

SUGAR COOKIES

Makes 12 to 15 cookies

2 vegan buttery sticks, at room temperature

3/4 cup sugar

1 teaspoon vanilla extract

2 teaspoons water

1/8 teaspoon lemon zest

1 teaspoon baking powder

2 cups flour

Preheat the oven to 375F. Line a baking sheet with parchment paper.

Cream together the buttery sticks, sugar, vanilla, water, and lemon zest. Then add the baking powder and flour.

Roll out dough to about 1/8-inch thickness. Cut with floured cookie cutter. Place on the baking sheet.

Bake for 8 to 10 minutes.

OATMEAL RAISIN COOKIES

Makes 12 cookies

1 1/2 cups raisins

2 1/2 vegan buttery sticks

3/4 cup brown sugar

1/2 cup sugar

1 1/2 teaspoon vanilla extract

1 teaspoon baking soda

1 teaspoon cinnamon

1/4 teaspoon nutmeg

1 1/2 cups flour

1/4 cup water

2 1/2 cups oatmeal

Preheat the oven to 375F. Line a cookie sheet with parchment paper.

To plump the raisins, place in a bowl and cover with water. Set aside.

Mix together the buttery sticks, sugars, and vanilla. Add the baking soda, cinnamon, nutmeg, flour, and water and mix well. Stir in the oats.

Drain the raisins and stir into the batter.

Use a tablespoon measure and drop by the spoonful onto the cookie sheet. Bake for 12 minutes.

NONGENDER SPECIFIC GINGER PEOPLE

Makes about 3 dozen cookies, depending on the size

1/2 cup vegan butter

1/2 cup sugar

1/2 cup brown sugar

1 cup molasses

2 teaspoons baking soda

1/2 teaspoon cloves

1 teaspoon cinnamon

2 teaspoons ground ginger

1 teaspoon sea salt

4 cups flour

1 cup water

WE LOVED MAKING these during the holidays almost as much as we loved the reaction to the name we gave our ginger people!

Preheat the oven to 375F. Line a cookie sheet with parchment paper.

Cream together the butter, sugars, and molasses. Add baking soda, cloves, cinnamon, ginger, salt, and 2 cups of flour. Add the water and the remaining flour, half a cup at a time. Roll out the dough to 1/4-inch thickness.

Bake for 10 to 15 minutes depending on the size and thickness.

CHOCOLATE CHIP COOKIE BARS

Makes 16 cookies

2 vegan buttery sticks, at room temperature

3/4 cup sugar

3/4 cup brown sugar

2 teaspoons vanilla extract

1 tablespoon water

2 1/4 cups flour

1/2 teaspoon sea salt

1 teaspoon baking soda

1/2 teaspoon baking powder

1 1/2 cups vegan chocolate chips

Preheat the oven to 350F. Prepare a 9" x 12" 1/4 sheet cake pan.

Mix together buttery sticks, sugars, vanilla, and water until creamy. Add dry ingredients and mix until everything is incorporated. Add chocolate chips and mix for 1 minute. Do not overmix once the chips are added.

Smooth the batter in the pan. Bake for 25 to 30 minutes. Cookies will appear to be undercooked but this is okay!

Allow the cookies to cool for 10 minutes before cutting into bars.

FUDGE COOKIES

Makes 8 cookies

Vegan Buttermilk

1/3 cup soymilk

1/2 teaspoon apple cider vinegar

1 teaspoon vanilla extract

Fudge Cookies

1 cup unbleached flour

1/8 teaspoon sea salt

1/4 teaspoon baking soda

1/3 cup vegan butter

1/2 cup cocoa powder

2/3 cup sugar

1/3 cup brown sugar

Preheat oven to 350F. Line a cookie sheet with parchment paper.

Mix the soymilk, vinegar, and vanilla and set aside to acidulate.

Combine flour, salt, and soda and set aside.

Melt the butter in a saucepan. Remove from heat, stir in the cocoa powder and the sugars. Add the buttermilk and mix well. Stir in the flour. Drop by tablespoonful onto the cookie sheet.

Bake for 8 to 10 minutes. Allow cookies to cool before removing from the cookie sheets.

Chocolate Chip
Cookie Bars

WHOOPIE PIES

Makes 32 pieces or 16 pies

Whoopie Pies

2 cups flour

1/4 cup cocoa powder

1 teaspoon baking powder

1 teaspoon baking soda

1/2 teaspoon sea salt

1 cup sugar

1/2 cup canola oil

1 cup water

2 teaspoon vanilla extract

1 cup soy milk

Cream Filling

4 vegan buttery sticks

5 cups powdered sugar

2 teaspoons vanilla extract

THIS CREAM FILLING is used for all these whoopie pies as well as our crème filled cupcakes. The recipe makes three to four times what you will need. But, it needs to be made in a big batch because you need the volume in the bowl so that it will whip up light and fluffy. You can freeze whatever you don't use for your next batch or for cream filled cupcakes.

Preheat the oven to 350F. Line a cookie sheet with parchment paper.

Add all the dry ingredients to the bowl of a stand mixer, fitted with a paddle attachment, and mix together. Add the canola oil, water, vanilla, and soy milk. Mix on low until smooth.

For each whoopee pie, scoop up 1/8 cup of batter and place on the cookie sheet.

Bake for 10 minutes. Allow to cool before filling.

To make the Cream Filling, add the buttery sticks to the bowl of your stand mixer. Alternatively, use a hand mixer. Whip at high speed until fluffy. This will take 10 to 15 minutes. The butter will get lighter in color as you go. Add sugar and vanilla and whip until the sugar is fully incorporated, and the filling is smooth and creamy.

For a pumpkin variation, use 1 1/3 cups of canola oil, 3/4 can of pumpkin, 1 teaspoon of vanilla extract, and 1/3 cup of water. Mix well and fill your pies.

See a photo of Whoopie Pies on the back cover.

MAPLE WHOOPIE PIES

Makes 30 pieces or 15 pies

1/2 cup brown sugar

1/3 to 1/2 cup water

2 cups flour

1/2 teaspoon baking soda

1/2 teaspoon baking powder

3/4 cup maple syrup

1/2 cup canola oil

2 teaspoon maple flavoring
(I like Frontier Coop Brand)

Preheat the oven to 325F. Line a cookie sheet with parchment paper.

In a small bowl, add the brown sugar in the water. It is important to make sure the sugar is dissolved completely for a smooth batter.

To the bowl of a stand mixer or, if using a hand mixer, to a mixing bowl, add the flour, baking soda, and baking powder. Add the dissolved brown sugar, and water, canola oil, and maple flavoring. Mix on low until smooth.

For each whoopie pie, scoop up 1/8 cup of batter and place on the cookie sheet.

Bake for 10 to 12 minutes. Allow to cool before filling.

LEMON COOKIE BARS

Makes 16 cookies bars

1 cup vegan butter

1 cup sugar

1 teaspoon vanilla extract

3 1/3 cup flour

1/2 teaspoon sea salt

1/2 teaspoon baking soda

1 teaspoon baking powder

2 lemons, zested and juiced

Preheat the oven to 350F.

In a mixing bowl, cream together the butter, sugar, and vanilla. Add the flour, sea salt, baking soda, baking powder, lemon juice, and zest. Mix until everything is incorporated.

Pour the batter to a lasagna pan and press it down. Use the back of a spoon to smooth the top.

Bake for 20 minutes. Allow to cool before cutting into bars.

Cream Filled Cupcakes

CREAM FILLED CUPCAKES

Makes 30 cupcakes

1/2 cup vegan butter

3/4 cup sugar

1/4 cup brown sugar

2 teaspoons vanilla extract

1 cup soy milk

2 1/2 cups flour

1/4 cup cocoa powder

2 1/2 teaspoons baking powder

1/2 teaspoon sea salt

Cream Filling, recipe on page 78

WHEN WE CAME up with our whoopie pie filling, we decided it was time to veganize a favorite childhood afterschool snack.

Preheat the oven to 350F. Line a muffin tin with cupcake liners.

In a mixing bowl, cream together the butter, sugar, brown sugar, and vanilla. Add the remaining ingredients and mix until smooth.

Using an ice cream scooper, fill each well up to the edge of the liner. Bake for 25 to 30 minutes.

Allow the cupcakes to cool but not completely before adding the filling.

It's time to fill the cupcakes. But, you may have to practice a few times to get it right. Too little and you won't have any filling; too much and the cupcake will crack. The good news is, the one that cracks is the one the baker will get to eat.

Place the frosting in frosting bag fitted with a large tip. Insert the tip into the center of the top of the cupcake, push it all the way down. Squeeze the frosting into the cupcake while slowly lifting the bag out.

PUMPKIN PIE

Makes 1 9" pie

1 pie crust, bottom only, recipe below

1 cup silken tofu

1 1/4 cup pumpkin

3/4 cup sugar

1/2 teaspoon salt

1/4 teaspoon ginger

1 teaspoon cinnamon

1 teaspoon flour

1/2 teaspoon vanilla extract

Preheat the oven to 375F. Place the pie crust in a pie plate and prebake for 15 minutes. Take the pie crust out of the oven and turn the heat up to 425F.

Drain the tofu. Add to the bowl of a food processor and puree until smooth. Add the tofu to the bowl of a stand mixer, or a mixing bowl if using a hand mixer, and add the rest of the ingredients. Mix until combined. Pour the pumpkin filling into the prebaked pie crust.

Bake for 35 minutes, or until the pie filling is set.

PIE CRUST

Makes 2 crusts, a top and a bottom

2 cups all-purpose flour

1 teaspoon sea salt

3/4 cup vegan butter

1/4 cup water

Put flour, sea salt, and vegan butter in a food processor and pulse until crumbly. Slowly add water until dough forms a ball. Remove and chill for 30 minutes.

Divide in half. Roll out each half to fit a 9" pie plate.

Squash Pie

Makes 1 9" pie

1 can squash

1/2 cup sugar

1/2 teaspoon salt

1 teaspoon ginger

1/2 teaspoon nutmeg

1/2 teaspoon cinnamon

1 teaspoon flour

1 cup silken tofu, pureed until smooth

1/2 teaspoon vanilla

1 pie crust, bottom only, recipe on facing page

OUR SON-IN-LOVE SWEARS there is a huge difference between pumpkin pie and squash pie, which is his favorite. We make this just for him every year at Thanksgiving even though we wonder if he really can tell the difference.

Preheat the oven to 375F. Place the pie crust in a pie plate and prebake for 15 minutes. Take the pie crust out of the oven and turn the heat up to 425F.

Drain the tofu. Add to the bowl of a food processor and puree until smooth. Add the tofu to the bowl of a stand mixer, or a mixing bowl if using a hand mixer, and add the rest of the ingredients. Mix until combined. Pour the pumpkin filling into the prebaked pie crust.

Bake for 35 minutes, or until the pie filling is set.

Strawberry Rhubarb Pie

Makes 1 9" pie

1 1/4 cups chopped rhubarb

2 1/2 cups sliced strawberries

1 cup sugar

3 tablespoons flour

1/2 teaspoon fresh lemon zest

1/2 teaspoon fresh lemon juice

1/2 teaspoon cinnamon

Pie crusts for top and bottom, recipe on facing page

Preheat oven to 425F. Line a cookie sheet lined with parchment or foil. You will bake your pie on this sheet because the pie may bubble over and this makes for easy cleanup!

Make pie crust and prepare a pie plate.

Mix all ingredients in a mixing bowl and immediately transfer to your prepared pie plate. Gently place the top crust over the mixture.

Bake for 10 minutes and then turn the oven temperature down to 350F and bake for another 40 to 50 minutes.

Bluebarbie Pie

BLUEBARBIE PIE

Makes 1 9" pie

2 cups chopped rhubarb

3 cups blueberries

1 1/4 cups sugar

2 tablespoons flour

1/2 teaspoon allspice

1/8 teaspoon salt

1 tablespoon fresh lemon juice

Pie crusts for top and bottom, recipe on page 82

MOM MADE THIS pie every year during blueberry season in Maine and again for Thanksgiving. It's a holiday tradition in our home.

Preheat oven to 425F. Line a cookie sheet lined with parchment or foil. You will bake your pie on this sheet because the pie may bubble over and this makes for easy cleanup!

Make pie crust and prepare a pie plate.

Mix all ingredients in a mixing bowl and immediately transfer to your prepared pie plate. Gently place the top crust over the mixture.

Bake for 10 minutes and then turn the oven temperature down to 350F and bake for another 40 to 50 minutes.

SIMPLE APPLE PIE

Makes 1 9" pie

4 apples, any variety

4 Granny Smith apples

3/4 cup sugar

1 teaspoon cinnamon

Pie crusts for top and bottom, recipe on page 82

Preheat the oven to 425F. Prepare your pie crust.

Peel and core the apples. Place in a large mixing bowl. Add sugar and cinnamon and gently mix to coat the apples.

Place the bottom crust in the pie plate. Add the filling into the crust and cover with the top crust. Cut 2 to 4 slits in the pie.

Bake for 10 minutes, turn the oven down to 350F and bake for 45 to 50 minutes.

DUTCH APPLE PIE

Makes 1 9" pie

3/4 cup oats

3/4 cup flour

3/4 cup brown sugar

1/3 cup melted vegan butter or coconut oil

Pie crusts for bottom, recipe on page 82

Want to make a Dutch apple pie? Combine the oats, flour, brown sugar, and butter or coconut oil. Skip the top crust and sprinkle this mixture over the apples instead.

Bake for 10 minutes at 425F, then turn the oven down to 350F and bake for 45 to 50 minutes.

CHOCOLATE CREAM PIE

Makes 1 9" pie

1/3 cup flour

1/3 cup sugar

2 cups soy creamer

1 tablespoon vanilla extract

1 cup vegan dark chocolate chips

1 graham cracker pie crust

Place the flour and sugar in a saucepan and whisk together. Add the soy creamer, vanilla, and chocolate chips. Heat over medium, whisking constantly. When the mixture starts to boil, turn the heat down to low. Continue whisking until it starts to thicken, about 5 minutes.

Pour into the prepared graham cracker crust. Let cool. Refrigerate for 2 hours before serving.

PUMPKIN COFFEE CAKE

Makes 1 9" x 9" Coffee Cake

Coffee Cake

2 cups flour

1 teaspoon baking powder

1 teaspoon baking soda

1/2 cup sugar

1/2 cup brown sugar

2 teaspoons cinnamon

1/2 teaspoon ginger

3/4 cup canola oil

1/2 can pumpkin

1 teaspoon vanilla extract

1/3 cup water

Topping

1/2 cup flour

1/3 cup brown sugar

1 teaspoon cinnamon

1/4 cup vegan butter, at room temperature

Preheat oven to 350F. Grease the bottom of a 9" x 9" cake pan.

Add all cake ingredients to the bowl of a stand mixer, or a mixing bowl, if using a hand mixer. Mix on medium until smooth.

Pour the batter into the cake pan and use the back of a spoon to smooth the top.

Make topping by combining the flour, sugar, cinnamon, and butter. Sprinkle it over the top of the coffee cake. Bake for 35 minutes.

Chocolate
Cream Pie

APPLE CAKE

Makes 1 9" x 9" Apple Cake

Cake

1 1/4 cups sugar

1/2 cup vegan butter

1 teaspoon vanilla extract

2 1/2 cups flour

2 1/2 teaspoons
baking powder

1/2 teaspoon sea salt

1/4 teaspoon nutmeg

1 1/2 teaspoon cinnamon

1 cup unsweetened soy milk

2 cups finely diced apples,
about 3 apples

Glaze

1 cup powdered sugar

1 teaspoon vegan butter,
melted

2 tablespoon soy milk

1/4 teaspoon cinnamon

THIS CAKE CAN crumble when you try to remove it from the pan, so I like to serve it in the pan that it is baked in.

Preheat the oven to 350F. Grease the bottom and sides of a 9" x 9" pan.

In the bowl of a stand mixer, or a mixing bowl if using a hand mixer, cream together the sugar, vegan butter, and vanilla until combined. Add the flour, baking powder, sea salt, nutmeg, cinnamon and soy milk. Mix on med for 3 minutes.

Use a spatula to fold in the apples.

Pour batter into prepared pan and bake for 55 minutes.

Make the glaze by mixing all the glaze ingredients together, using a whisk to make it perfectly smooth.

When the cake is cool, pour the glaze over the top and serve.

Chocolate Chip Bundt Cake

Makes 1 Bundt Cake or 12 mini-cakes

1/2 cup vegan butter

3/4 cup sugar

3/4 cup brown sugar

2 1/2 cups flour

2 teaspoons baking powder

1 teaspoon baking soda

1 cup vanilla soy milk

1 1/2 teaspoons vanilla extract

1/4 cup water

1 1/2 cups vegan chocolate chips

MOM ALWAYS LIKED to make Bundt cakes, so this cake reminds me of my childhood.

Preheat the oven to 350F. Generously grease and flour a Bundt pan or 12 mini Bundt pans. Gently tap the bottom of the pan to remove excess flour.

Place the butter and sugars into the bowl of your stand mixer, or a mixing bowl if using a hand mixer. Mix on medium until smooth.

Add the flour, baking powder, baking soda, soy milk, vanilla, and water. Mix on low to medium until well combined. Add the chocolate chips and mix on low for a minute.

Add the batter to your Bundt pan or minis and bake for 55 to 60 minutes, or 35 to 40 minutes for the mini-cakes.

Sweet Potato Brownies

Makes 16 Brownies

2 1/2 cups mashed sweet potatoes, about 2 medium sized potatoes

2 1/2 cups flour

2 cups sugar

1/2 teaspoon baking powder

1/2 teaspoon baking soda

2 teaspoons cinnamon

1/4 cup cocoa powder

1 cup canola oil

1/2 cup vanilla soy milk

1 tablespoon vanilla

1/4 cup molasses

1 cup vegan mini chocolate chips

SWEET POTATOES ARE one of our grandchildren's favorite foods, so we created this special sweet treat for them.

Peel the sweet potatoes and cut into small pieces. Place in a pan, cover with water, and cook until soft. Drain, mash, and set aside to cool.

Preheat the oven to 350F. Grease a 9" x 13" pan or line with parchment paper.

Add the rest of the ingredients (but not the chocolate chips) to a mixing bowl. Add cooled sweet potatoes and mix until smooth.

Pour batter into the pan and smooth the top and bake for 30 to 35 minutes.

As soon as you remove the pan from the oven, sprinkle the chocolate chips evenly over the top.

As the chocolate chips melt, carefully spread them over the top. Allow the brownies to cool completely before cutting into squares.

Lemon Bundt
Mini-Cakes

Lemon Bundt Cake

Makes 1 Bundt Cake or 12 mini-cakes

1 1/4 cups sugar

1/2 cup vegan butter

1 teaspoon vanilla extract

2 1/2 cups flour

2 1/2 teaspoon
baking powder

1/2 teaspoon sea salt

2 large lemons, zested
and juiced

1 cup unsweetened soy milk

Glaze

1 cup powdered sugar

1 teaspoon vegan butter,
melted

1 tablespoon water

Lemon zest and juice

Preheat the oven to 350F. Grease and flour the bottom and sides of a Bundt pan or mini-Bundt pan. I love my mini bee-hive Bundt pan for this cake.

In the bowl of a stand mixer, or a mixing bowl if using a hand mixer, cream together the sugar, butter, and vanilla until creamy. Add the flour, baking powder, sea salt, 1 1/2 tea-spoons lemon zest, 2 tablespoons lemon juice, and soy milk.

Mix on medium until the batter is smooth, 4 to 5 minutes. Pour the batter into the prepared pan and bake for 50 minutes, or 30 minutes for mini-cakes.

Make the glaze by mixing all the glaze ingredients together, using a whisk to make it perfectly smooth.

When the cake is cool, pour the glaze over the top and serve.

CHEESECAKE

Makes 1 Cheesecake

Graham Cracker Pie Crust

1 14 oz. box of
graham crackers

1/4 cup vegan butter

Cheesecake

1 teaspoon agar flakes

1/2 cup water

1 12.3 oz. box Mori-Nu extra
firm silken tofu

2 8 oz. packages Tofutti
cream cheese, at room
temperature

3/4 cup sugar

1 teaspoon vanilla extract

1 1/2 teaspoons fresh
lemon juice

1/4 teaspoon salt

I AM LISTING the brand of vegan cream cheese and tofu that I use because I have never made this with any other brands, so I can't guarantee that the texture and taste will be the same using anything else. Feel free to experiment with your own favorite brands. And if you don't want to make your own crust, go ahead and buy a premade crust.

To make the crust, add the graham crackers and butter to the food processor. Process for 3 to 5 minutes, until the crackers are crumbly and the butter is mixed in. Transfer to a pie plate and press into the bottom and sides.

Place agar and water in a saucepan to soak. Set aside for 30 minutes.

Heat the agar over medium heat, whisking constantly for 2 to 3 minutes until the mixture thickens.

Preheat the oven to 350F.

While the agar is cooling, drain the tofu and process it in a food processor until very creamy, the longer the better. You cannot overdo this step.

Add the cooled agar and remaining ingredients to the food processor and mix for 10 minutes. Scrape down the sides and process for another 5 minutes.

Pour batter into crust, using the back of a spoon to smooth the top and bake for 30 to 40 minutes.

How do you know when cheesecake is done? To test for doneness, very lightly tap the top of the cheesecake with your finger. If the "skin" is firm, it's done. If it sticks to your finger, cook for another 5 minutes.

NOTES

ABOUT THE AUTHOR

PATTI DANN IS the founder and owner of Café Indigo, a bakery renowned for its delectable vegan cakes. Patti's journey into the world of vegan food began with her desire to find a delicious wedding cake for her daughter and soon to be son-in-love. It wasn't long before she realized that the only way to find a vegan cake to meet her exacting standards was to convert an old family recipe. Her success at creating a vegan carrot cake, one that everyone could enjoy, was the impetus for Patti to open her bakery. Today, her much-sought-after carrot, chocolate, and lemon poppy seed cakes are available at Whole Foods and fine markets across the country under the Café Indigo label. In addition to multiple local awards for their high quality and irresistible taste, Patti was named New Hampshire's Women Owned Business of the Year and her famous cakes received The Best of New Hampshire award. And now, Patti has created this wonderful cookbook, filled with recipes from her café along with new favorites, providing you with the best of what we know as *vegan comfort food.*